J. Brookes

The Dresden Cantata

Also by J. Brookes:

Dusting the Bin
The Deafening Nose
From the School of Mulligan and Rooke
Nobby: Prince of Wales

J. BROOKES
THE DRESDEN CANTATA

Published by Square Books 2008

Cover illustration, "The Other" by Naïve John,
reproduced with kind permission of the artist
(copyright retained)

Some of these poems have previously appeared in *The New Welsh Review,*
Orbis (Welsh issue), *Planet, Poetry Wales, Square, The Wide Skirt* and
The Yellow Crane

Printed by

Cambrian Printers
Llanbadarn Road
Aberystwyth
Ceredigion
SY23 3TN

The publisher acknowledges the financial support of
the Welsh Books Council

Square Books
2 Richmond House
Richmond Road
Cardiff CF24 3AR

www.squarepublishing.com

A CIP record for this title is available from the British Library

ISBN 978-0-9555492-1-2

Contents

The Dance

I have this picture of an ardent suitor
marking his dance-card in advance
and letting himself in at the end
for a knock round the face with a fan
and a slow walk home alone.

Dance-cards? Fans? Wrong scene;
I am at the bar of a Wetherspoons
pretending to read the Echo
and you are busy sorting cutlery
yonder in the field of mustard pots.

But my heart has gone to a ball,
it is putting its little pointy toe out,
prinked and pomaded it is feinting
and falling back for you to step,
one, two, and forward again, banquets
and golden carriages to ensue.

Marry, but that's a merry tableau
I've got going on down there
between the breastbone and left arm,
between the left arm and where you stand
pleating paper napkins into swans,
or maybe fans, I can't see from here.

Moon

Stepping to the pub on a stormy night
heart and head all upside down
the clouds fell suddenly apart
and there the moon was in her nightgown.

Hallo J... she said and smiled
serenely down to where I stood
to watch her standing bright and cold
against the sky and rushing cloud.

And that was that, the gap closed up
and a half forgotten scene was gone
of a small boy at a water-stoop
with a statue of the Virgin on.

Conditioner

Now the blonde is growing back
after the small disaster of brunette
which means you'll be in bloom
in time for spring. See,

by the bath, *Autumn Rêve*
is being crowded-out and *Party Girl!*
and *On the Town* are being upturned
and squeezed again. All things

gutter and go out, then come round
in a different light, or, as the blusher
put it to the pot of glitter,

if the shoots are showing through
how long the full-on curling tongs,
pink Stetsons, Dusty Springfield songs?

A Little Tornado

Occasional independent breezes
had been crossing and re-crossing
all afternoon in the trees,
when out of the blue
a correct in all particulars
two foot tall tornado
stepped out of a litterbin
and set off round the rose garden.

Everyone was enchanted
by the mute phenomenon,
pointing and calling to each other
as it waltzed about
like the ghost of a spin-dryer
in an upended coal scuttle,
some averring that it was a model
and radio-controlled, and others
knowing it was not.

And so it danced, now on the lawn,
now on the crazy paving bridge
and now up where the prams stood
around an ice-cream van,
and then a little dog
that had lost the trail of a rat
came trotting over
and broke its concentration
by sticking its big nose in,

at which it sat down hard
like a child surprised,
to whom we ran
with our arms held wide.

A Wasp

A wasp, astride the high-horse of itself,
rides the updraughts of the afternoon
and steps in through my open window
to marvel at the wonders of my book,
my shirt, my ear. Inch long

outrider of some city-state
up a tree or sealed beneath a gutter,
I could raise this book and with a swipe
unpick your noisy yellow stitch
from the long tapestry of the afternoon,

and would, but for the picture that I have
of some wasp-waisted Isolde where she sits
with unattended needlework or mandolin,
pale for the shouts and lamps of your return,
full of the wonders you have seen.

Encomium

Now I shall speak of lofty and eternal things
like the care the girl downstairs displays for the aunt
who blew her cat and other things clean through a wall
lighting a Calor gas heater a winter or so ago,
for she has not allowed her relative to fall
into the hands of the Geriatric Residential Services
where she would not be allowed to keep cats,
but has instead busied herself at all hours
washing and pegging out her auntie's bloomers,
renewing bus-passes and going to the shops
for cabbages and cakes and Kit-e-Kat,
and all this as quietly as the sun crossing the road,
without expectation of reward or praise
but because this is just the way the universe goes.

Pre-Raphaelite Portraits

You're waiting at table in Holborn tea rooms
or putting hems in other people's underwear
when the paint-smelling gentlemen come in:
My dear Hunt, never in all my born days...

What they want is your kiss-swollen mouths
to which a piece of porphyry or stem of rue
is pressed, *in pensive or distracted mood*,
as Bulwer Lytton has it when he calls.

Bulwer old boy... park the topper... wine?
the tantalus is opened with a little silver key,
the scuttle is upended over the grate:
Kitty, it's Lytton, you may as well step down.

You're letting a seam out in a tea-gown
or writing *Dearest Aggie...* to a friend,
slowly your blue-veined hands are moving:
Doctor Monkton recommended Folkstone.

Bulwer's turn-ups are close to burning:
Algernon's living with Watts... Dadd's insane...
and now you are going out to catch the post,
the snow is deep, your consumption galloping.

Mini-Roundabout

One minute, there they are, driving to school
with the taste of toothpaste in their mouths,
and the next, what do you know, Mother
has climbed a mini-roundabout

and turned the car over. Off-side up
it hangs, emitting smoke, no, steam,
in a steady stream from low on its brown,
portioned and perforated belly, beyond which

men are picking children out, still holding
projects and pink umbrellas. Soon
the ambulances and the police, but for now

they stand watching Mother being released,
wondering if this means they'll miss school,
one checking her new shoes for scuffs.

Ants

According to The Bumper Book for Boys
armies of ants regularly marched through remote places
leaving only the picked-clean bones
of grazing cattle. And if there'd always be

a girl in jodhpurs and a clean white shirt
whom circumstances would pin in the ants' path
until the handsome Anglo Saxon ranger
swept her to safety at last on his pommel,

the central fact of the story was not the ants,
the girl in jodhpurs or the handsome ranger,
but all the horror-struck natives fleeing
with pitiful things like babies and bags of beans.

Easter Sunday

In chapels like upturned boats
and in cathedrals that float
over dower house and close
a hundred thousand sermons end

on an upbeat note. At home
I stand at the kitchen window
with bacon and the heating down
and feel the caveman in me grin

as he begins unwinding skins
at winter's end. And just as those
who huddled in their pelts and froze
a million orbits of the sun ago

gave thanks, so I give thanks
for winter's what it ever was
and still demands its sacrifice
of hopeless overdose or madhouse

though boilers hum and over all
the ever watchful satellites
look down. But now the earth
is warm and full of shoots, swifts

are shrilling round the house
and, can it be, high in the stacks,
the dream of love in a gull's eye?
Most things are happy just to be,

I never knew a beast that needed
immortality, so while the upbeat
Easter sermons reach Amen
and bells ring out to celebrate

the Son returning in his glory,
flower and fruit of that bare tree
without a root, I stand and watch
a spray of bluetits come to feed

noisily on peanuts that I hung,
and see once more the miracle is done
for I have bacon and a cup of tea
and there are buds upon the tree.

Daisies

I sing the feverfew and sneezewort
that blow upon the wastelands
for girls who dance all night to lose
their underwear among. Yarrow

and scentless mayweed I also praise
for they are not of low esteem
though dwell the hypodermic
bottle-cap and durex at their stem.

Ancestor

Great Grandfather was a tramp
- just pushed off and left
his Edwardian family
to cope with the scandal

of being abandoned.
I used to picture him
sitting in a sunlit hedge
frying lark eggs in a hubcap

or leaving twig-hieroglyphics
outside the big houses
as tramps did back then,
though in fact he was dead

of drink and neglect
in a Paddington dosshouse
before I could picture anything.
He was a poet, really

my aunt recently said,
and I like to believe it
though the evidence is thin
since all he left

was an old perambulator
full of newspapers and tins,
still, he was an ancestor
and I push my pram after him.

The Aunts

Pine-clad down the singing chapel
another uncle that I barely knew
flows out into the afternoon
to start a new life underground
or scattered somewhere dear to him.
The organ wheezes as we step
from creaking pews into the sun
where someone waves, and over there
mob-handed stand the merry aunts
plotting pubs and latest trains.
So, in the City Arms saloon
we drink away the afternoon
toasting the uncle newly dead
and those of us still pushing on
till suddenly it's later than we thought,
the aunts and cousins behind prams
are waving back while running hard
for waiting trains, and later
in the corner of a crowded carriage
I look out at the passing darkness
and think about the unknown uncles
falling like a view of trees
and of the aunts, now newly strange,
rising behind them like a mountain range.

The Dropped Nail

This is the nail that got mislaid,
that dropped to the ground with a little shriek
and rolled away
while the other nails
went snugly in
to start interesting and useful lives
holding up shelves.
                    This is the nail
that sat in the gutter
among the dogshit and the litter
and almost passed out with panic:
what else is a nail to do
but sit in a wall
with other nails
smoking a pipe
and wearing overalls?

And while all the other nails
are enjoying works parties
and forming lottery syndicates,
                          this is the nail
that from its blister pack was drawn
kite marked, keen and level-headed
and quite as ready to hold things together
as any other,
                the nail
that now lies in the gutter
oxidising slowly,
losing its glamour,
growing bitter and twisted,
with nothing better to do
than burst the odd bicycle tyre
and once give a small dog tetanus
as it came gambolling joyfully through.

Bonny Youth

A powerboat called Bonny Youth
with a flash plastic playboy at the wheel,
and just to port, true to its last gun turret,
a destroyer of a class its owner will know.

And Bonny Youth is to the destroyer
as a large red kitten to small grey mouse,
really rather scaring the Old Man
in the quietly humming operations room.

See him with his brightest lieutenants
trying to hold his nerve in the face
of the teeth that keep filling his portholes,
the fixed stare, the hair's shining peaks.

Schnapphund Podspringer

A little red dog
about the size of two oranges
follows you home.
         It's
an ugly looking thing
that could have escaped
from a cancer research laboratory
or fallen out of a novel
set among canal folk
on the Dnieper.
         You
bring it in
and give it the tin of dog food
you were saving for hedgehogs,
and then, just out of interest,
go to your *Wonderful World of Dogs* book
and look up dogs with rat-like tails,
wrinkled brows, double chins,
smoking pipes and wearing
sailors hats.
         To your delight
you find that, without doubt,
it's a pure bred Schnapphund Podspringer,
worth its weight (8.5 ounces)
in gold.

You look at the Schnapphund Podspringer
and the Schnapphund Podspringer looks at you,

then an accordion is produced
and one or other of you goes out for a bottle of whisky.

The Dresden Cantata

Here comes the Dresden Cantata
says the master of the crematorium
as the cortege, spitting pebbles, nears.

This morning he's had Loquacious Brat,
the theme tune to *Gone to Earth*
and an atonal sonata for piano and flute.

After the Dresden Cantata he's got
a barber shop quartet, the Hayseeds,
In Thy Bosom Now I Rest, and *Froot!*

The Lovers
(With a nod to Edward Thomas)

When the team turned at the field's end
and the man on the elm looked away
I lifted the wire and took her hand
and we ducked in. On leaves we lay

for an hour or so, as the horses came
to the end of the row and the man
on the elm and the man with the team
spoke a bit and the team moved on,

and then I took her hand and we
slipped through the wire and into the clay,
for she had an aunt with a waiting tea
and I was due in France next day.

Mr. O'Brien

Late morning, walking to the dole,
I said *hallo* to fat Mr. O'Brien
who set off with me, walking along
in his big new canary-yellow boots.

Mr. O'Brien had a bag of sandwiches
and as he ate he threw the paper down:
Litter I said loudly as we walked,
Yes, said Mr. O'Brien and walked on.

Just then Sharon came round the corner
pushing her new boyfriend
who'd recently had his foot amputated:
he's got other problems too, she said.
.

Her boyfriend was up to his left index finger
when I remembered where I should be
and set off at a run: *Where are you going?*
shouted Sharon and Mr. O'Brien.

*Yonder, over Jordan, where the poor
are passing through the eyes of needles,*
I said, and pointed to the dole office
where the clock was looking grim.

Oh, the poor... said Mr. O'Brien,
Oh, the poor... said Sharon,
her boyfriend said *hypertension,
arteriosclerosis, fatty degeneration...*

Trish

Daddy didn't love his girl,
Daddy loved his girl too much
and now she lives in a hospital
does poor old Trish.

They've given up, they've given up
teaching her to cook and paint,
not cheat at bingo, steal fags
or tuck her skirt into her pants.

When Daddy comes she's going home
to ride a pony round and round
and be his girl, his golden girl:
'Look Daddy…' she will cry
and jump the little horse for joy.

The birthdays come, the birthdays go,
now fifty candles mark the day
and she has whiskers long and grey
and something else they dare not say
that's eating her insides away.

For every happy life there's one
that moons about a corridor
dumb to say just what's gone wrong,
dumb to say and dumb to say
who stole her little life away
and gave her only Trish to be,
only Trish, eternally,
and that seems very sad to me.

Night & Day

My boozy friends have blown or lie
where sleep has taken them and snore
like heavy and unfastened doors
and now, as sure as night and day
take turn and turn-about, the dawn
will want to know the reason why.

I hear my neighbour getting up,
first trains approaching down the line
with breakfast chefs and cleaners on,
and now the dull diversions of the day
in canteen kitchens and shop floors
seem all that there has ever been.

Day hides night and night hides day,
each completely, till the other come,
and as my fellow shipwrecks groan,
raise their boots and snore again,
dawn puts its sempiternal question,
bold and watery and common.

Reg and Ron and Roy and Ray
marooned among the cans and ashtrays
as things outside get underway,
why had we not the wisdom to foresee
that having battled dark and won
the sun would rise and we'd be done?

Photograph of an American Indian

One of his eyes
has an inward look
as though he were observing
prairies, larchwoods
and salmon rivers
in his head.

The date is 1891
and this is
One-Foot-Running
boldly squaring up
to the camera
in a mouldy frockcoat.

An old, sepia-brown photo
in a book called
Wounded Knee: The Aftermath
or something,
it is a face
unused to focusing

on its own humiliation,
though soon enough, no doubt,
The Society
for the Advancement of
will be passing on
a pair of spectacles.

Greybeards

When the children ran out
everyone dropped what they were doing
and crowded to the windows
crying: *come back
and continue your studies,
this thing is unique and delicate,
full of switches and gadgets...*
but the children shook their heads,
they said it didn't matter,
that, anyway, they had their own,
and ran away laughing.

And when they came back
saying how they'd been mistaken
and that it *was* the only one,

everyone inside
was pleased to teach them
everything

except where they kept the other one
in which they left
when it was time to.

Clifton Street, Cardiff

I sit in a cafe on Clifton Street
and stir my tea and look about,
another man of forty eight
in Oxfam shirt and overcoat.

Outside, through the usual rain,
the usual traffic bumper to bumper,
inside, a steaming silver urn
wrinkles the face of Miss November.

The rain falls, the urn steams...
O what have I done with beautiful Time
for calendars pass as though a thumb
were riffled down the edge of them

and soon, soon, the nursing home,
the toast-rack and the sugar-tongs,
soon, soon the walking frame,
the Lennon & McCartney sing-songs.

Along the street two dumper trucks
are inching up to where a gang
of demolition men are making bricks
with a steel ball on a chain.

The street renews, decays, renews,
and will do till there is no call
for pegs or birthday cards or shoes,
no call for plugs or stamps at all.

And when one day they come across
me face down in my morning porridge
and Matron, with a look at Nurse,
wheels me quietly to the fridge,

there'll be a man on Clifton Street
who stirs his tea and looks about,
who sighs, and lights a cigarette,
and smokes awhile and stubs it out,

then seeing that the sky has put
a hanky to its streaming face,
with shoulders back steps boldly out
for fuses, glue or pudding rice.

Three Short Rings

Three short rings, your old signal,
and I'm flying downstairs with a song
in my heart and my heart in my mouth
to see you there, slowly becoming

somebody else. Retrieving my face
from the floor, I try to attend
to this neighbour, salesman or friend,
but all I hear is the blood in my head

saying *Three short rings... and not you...*
as though all that weren't long ago
and three short rings meant any more
than one short ring, or two, or four.

The Garden City of Milton Keynes

I will arise and go now, and go to Milton Keynes,
And a small town house buy there, of brick and breezeblock made,
Patio decking I will have, and a line for a row of jeans
And there I'll live with Jennifer, little Ben and Jade.

And I shall have a lease there of nine and ninety years,
A storeman's post in Comet on an out-of-town estate,
And peace will be the Bendix and the Hoover on the stairs,
And peace the Mr. Whippy's song beyond the garden gate.

I will arise and go now, for always night and day
I hear the Black & Decker and the Flymo call to me
While I stand in the peatbog or by the ocean grey,
I hear them on the radio and see them on TV.

St. Fagans

With one resentful eye a rootling boar
of some antique and noble line
observes another 3b pick its way
with little shrieks and steadying hands
to an Iron Age ideal home. Inside,

a Celt with braided orange hair
and home-made coat, pops half a Kit-Kat
on a beam and clears her throat
as 3b crackle smoky-bacon crisps
and look about with thoughtful frowns

at querns, at blackened earthenware
and drinking horns. Outside again
and forty projects underway
the boys are high on ancient warfare
and whoop away for Wagon-Wheels

and waiting coaches, but the girls
come dawdling down beside the Celt
pushing her Muddy Fox along the lane
and speak of an older sister's braided hair,
a camping break in Tenby when it rained all week.

Potwasher

That potwasher some famous poet once said
he would certainly have been if he hadn't been a poet,

I met him today in the Market Diner. The spit
of the famous one's non-famous alter ego he was,

right down to the hole in the shoe and the space
on the shelf for the Nobel Prize. I watched him

lathering plates and towelling them dry, this man
quite without other resources, born to wash pots

if poetry doesn't give him wing... as it was put
by that Brodsky or Milosz whose poems *did* come.

Her Pottery

Back from night class with another turkey
she wonders why things always go awry
between her vision and the firing,
why so little that she makes
is worth admiring. Oddballs as they are,

these squat brown pots with fuzzy stripes,
these sagging pitchers with green spots
and spindly, leaning pale blue vases
that have come to colonise the house
good naturedly holding flowers, drawing pins

or bits of string, but I admire them,
perhaps because they always seem
more surprised and grateful to have been
brought into existence by her hands
than any Spode or Wedgwood that I've seen.

Killing the Dog

The dog got cancer and the rot
carried half her face off
in six months.

With growing squeamishness
we took her out,
first minus a cheek,
then an eye,
then half a nose,

till, finally, imagining
not long from then
a single shin-bone
or a set of teeth
chasing a red ball
through the trees,
we led her firmly downhill
to the vet.
     The needle
sank in through a patch
of shaved white skin
and she looked stung,

then, recognising that the tide
now washing in
and drumming through her head
was death,
she set up such a howl
we stopped our ears and wept
until she dropped.

Even the vet was shocked,
and the waiting room
when we walked back through
holding the lead
and identity disc
was stiff as wood
with faces, animal and human,
breathing hard
and watching us.

Killing the dog
was one of the last things
we did together,
and we did it so bravely
and so well
that walking back up the hill
it almost felt
we could go on together
for years and years.

Snowdon

Rising up Snowdon, watching the Llanberis fudge stalls
dwindle below, the lake unfolding like a handkerchief

and the red faces of climbers looming up from the path by the rails
as we clank over the tree-line, taking the Victorian route

up through the scree and the outcrops, past vertiginous drops
and dizzying crags, till we reach the tea-shop at the top

where I sit with a sandwich and someone's nan
who tells me about Walsall and her husband Stan

who's off her hands for a week in the home
and she just thought, *alright girl, do it while you can...*

Sex Cinema

A fraulein rolls a stocking on, a plumber leaves
backwards down the garden path, and now
in underwear she wonders how to spend the day
irritably tugging cut flowers out of water

then getting into bed alone. And that's our lot,
and none the worse for having been in reverse,
climax moving slowly through softening moans
to the glint in the eye, and from there to that

polite ...*ttimhcS uarF negromnetuG* as the door
closes on his smiling face, expunging their play,
right back to the hand-on-heart, without a blush,
it wasn't me, I wasn't there at all today...

A Walk in Cathays Cemetery

Owen Preece, hairy-eared old general practitioner
with your choir practice and Hillman Sunbeam,

and Ellen Rees, late of Radyr, with your chapped hands
and prizewinning jams, I picture you down there,

long off the bone and under your headstones,
both still *in sure and certain hope*...

after all those years, while upstairs in the sun
magpies tommy-gun among the holly trees

and bees like little bibles in their black and gold
move between stands of chapped hands and hairy ears.

Cathedral

Something there is that bores about cathedrals,
the coppiced close of long-forgotten stone
and gravel paths along which bishops come
solemnly sounding their bike-bells in the sun.

Something about the cat-flap in the studded door
and stepping through that weighs on me;
stupendous it might be, but it doesn't look likeable,
not something you'd want sleeping on the settee.

You can't have a conversation with a cathedral,
it's a one-way thing, your words will fall
on the deaf ears of prelates and primates and peers
sequestered in their niches on the stone-cold wall.

And look, over there, where a few pews have filled,
that place in the middle like a boxing ring
where the ancient rites and rituals still go on,
as though so small a fire could stoke so huge a thing.

No, something there is that leaves me cold,
that turns me round for the door and the sun
for one in The Old Cross or Mason's Arms
then back to the backstreets on the day return.

Caravan Site (St. Mary's Well Bay)

The dogs bark, the caravans move on
their moorings in the wind. Gypsy Queen,

Romany and Wanderer, each with a plot
of pansies, something hardy in a pot

by the door, and dustbin at the back.
And walking past, along the track

from Sully Island up to Lavernock,
the acres of them waiting under padlock

for flip-flopped summer in its funny hat
to bounce across the field and get

things going again, seem such emphatic
statements of the optimistic

that despite the wind and rain I stop
to take the place in, from the shuttered shop

still advertising Walls, to what looks like
a shower room maybe, or a laundry block,

as though there were some lesson I could learn
from Romany and Wanderer and Gypsy Queen

all going nowhere on their breezeblock wheels
but here, a turnip field beside the sea, in Wales.

Gypsies

Our mothers said we never should
and so we don't, but sometimes see
a huddle of your caravans drawn-up
with lurchers on the ends of chains
and washing strung to Keep Out signs.

And driving past towards the motorway
taxed and mortgaged firmly into life
we maybe wonder briefly at your lives
staked-out with buckets and jump leads
where A roads queue for roundabouts.

The vision goes, the burning oil drums
dwindle swiftly in the rear-view mirror
and office blocks where consoles wait
to feed the mortgage on the Beazer home
appear, like intimations of Eternity.

The settled life, the fixed address
postcoded in some leafy cul-de-sac,
and all the numbers that we add up to
verified, coldly approved and filed away,
these are the chains of the working day.

Truly, the blood of Man is wonderful
that turns from Payroll and Personnel
for the loan of a standpipe by the road
and a life as hard as a bailiff's writ,
light as a nosegay bought on the street.

Father

Mile End Road
receivers of stolen goods
you said, and even
when you were getting on

you had the upstart look
of the gutter kid
who gets to grammar school,
the charmer from nowhere

who marries well. Family trees
grow tall and wide
and you can't see much
for the leaves of Time

but I loved that dark
satiric vein you kept
that spoke of hungry blood
just down the line.

After your death
I got your poetry books
amongst which
was a jumble sale edition

of Thomas Campion
laboriously inscribed
from me to you
in 40 year old Quink,

and the much later
Selected Derek Mahon
which (blood will out)
I'd nicked, I think.

Echo

It hits the streets with the damp thud of a bale
and is either dispensed from a box on wheels

by a man with the voice of a crow, or it goes
with the gum and the Flake at a sweetshop till.

Once bought, it may be leafed through quickly
for *that* photo, or the pile-ups and break-ins

may be folded or rolled into pocket or bag
till the fag in the pub or digestives at home.

No sooner read and sheared of its coupons
and pull-outs of Babies and glowing Brides

it may take its place in the pile for the cat-tray
beside the pouffe, or knock about all afternoon

being torn and soaking up beer. Either way,
its Tomorrows are made with the pulp of Today.

Known, but not Wanted

Known, but not wanted... the radio returned.
Between the slip road and the bank of weeds
that lined it down to where it joined
the warbling northward motorway to Leeds

I stood, all thumb and loons and Mersey Sound,
frisked, but found clean. As satisfactory
as Leicestershire's constabulary would ever find
the jib of me, from lip to book of effing poetry,

the panda sped off to a call with the advice
to, *in future, keep it buttoned chum...*
And so I stuck my tongue out at them twice
for honour's sake, then lifted up my thumb

and there the memory ends, and would be gone
itself but for those four small words
suspended in the static of a distant afternoon,
known, but not wanted..., words for a squat in Leeds

to fall about at later over cider and a chillum,
but deepening as time went on, and darkening
till, thirty years from then they almost seem
my own time's final, dismal reckoning.

The Missionary Position

She went through the front door
like she expected it to be locked
and I heard her feet disappearing up the street
at the gallop.
　　　　　Listen, friend,
I'd long been planning this trip,
In my pocket was a one-way ticket
and tomorrow I'd be miles away
as teacher of Christian-based home economics
at Hyena Creek School for Orphans.
I was looking forward to it.

One can only be a banker for so long.
The house had been sold,
the children already in care
and she whom I'd wed all those years ago
had taken a bedsit in Poverty Square.
Sometimes you just know you're doing the right thing.

Now, alone in a mud hut
I write home by the light
of a hurricane lamp: *I live in fear,*
I think this place is my subconscious,
I miss you dear... using sperm
to stick on the bright,
glueless African stamp.

Or Else

Or else to up and chuck all this
and live in gumboots down a lane
with can-openers and camping-gas
and nettles round the caravan.

To up and off and be the sort
who late on snowy nights is seen
in knitted hat and army greatcoat
crossing fields he does not own.

It will be cold, the wind will whine,
the frost will spin, the moon will stare
and all the stars above will shine
like moth holes in old underwear,

and sometimes in my pull-down bed
beside an oil lamp's smoky flame
I'll take down the city A-Z
and bring to mind each friendly name.

*

The road not taken is the one
that comes to haunt us in the night
with its *perhaps I should have done...*
and *what if I'd decided that...?*

For if alone I lie at night
marooned among unfriendly farms
will I pull my dossbag tight
against Regret's goose-pimpled arms

and tremble for that foolish turn
taken where the road divides,
the one for going mad alone,
the other, bingo, free bus rides,

pedicare and tight new teeth
and all that *mustn't grumble* thing
until the fall or scalding bath
and then the geriatric wing?

*

But then, when nodding by the News
with Ovaltine and custard creams
and Matron bounces in and cries
Bedtime boys and girls, sweet dreams...

and plumps the cushions as I squeak
down halls of Pledge and Windowlene
that all lead to the Heart-Attack
and then the black cars in the rain,

will I not wish I'd chucked the telly
to live on toast and nettle wine,
shriven, saintly, somewhat smelly
in cords held up with baler-twine,

the sort a farmer comes across
like that prehistoric Alpine man,
frozen solid in a fosse
the wrong side of a Keep Out sign?

Visit

You've clearly had it, and my duty quickly done
I farewell awkwardly and step back out to where
your wife as thin as weeks of worry sits alone
with crumpled Kleenex in her velvet armchair,

apologise for something, smile and leave. The world goes on
and will do after we poor grave-sized things
have left for Thornhill in that weeping limousine,
when caterers have cleared the pies and chicken wings

and mates who thought they ought to and brought in
the Echo or the landlord's latest daft one-liner
have drawn new team lists up for skittles nights in town.
Momentous things up close can turn out minor

as funeral directors in a back room sipping tea
before the next hearse sighs along the bitumen and brakes
beside the tulips in the rain, and this is how it has to be
or how is that same someone dear who sat for weeks

next door beside an ashtray with the TV down
to pack your washed and ironed shirts for Age Concern,
advertise your fishing rods and honky-tonk LPs, then
go on coach tours, take up bingo again?

Thanks a Million

For the Welsh rugby captain carved out of coal,
for the Chinese combined calculator and address book,
for the signed (by Aunt Mabel) Collected Edith Sitwell,
for the cheeky *Happy Chopper* wind-up plastic cock,

for the personalised beechwood gear-stick knob,
for the six sessions on a sunbed plus *Tan Safely* CD,
for the year's subscription to the Caravan Club,
for the framed photo of a niece receiving her degree,

for the wipe-clean vinyl apron with fanny and tits,
for the Trusthouse Forte (Hounslow) bargain weekend break,
for the two Classic FM *Music for Lovers* cassettes,
for the baseball cap with a turd on the peak,

for the book of postcards of video installations,
for the walking stick with the brass duck handle,
for the calendar featuring the United Nations,
for the Wordsworth edition of a long novel by Stendhal,

for the video of *The Cook, The Thief, His Wife and Her Lover*,
for the travelling onyx toothbrush stand and soap dish,
for the hand-knitted telephone directory cover,
for the *Fossil Starter Kit* of a trowel and a dead fish.

Lottery

Woke to our hearing, fireworks, the day the lottery was born,
but saw nothing, the sun already having risen.

That afternoon we bought tickets, dripping with luck,
and walked up through the rec. and the graveyard

and down to the river, secret and elated, counting our stash.
That night we watched as someone else's luck came in,

and next week, next week was when we found that car-struck dog
outside the Claude, the one whose convulsive little body

I picked up and placed to die in the gutter, its two eyes
popping out like something being amazed in Disney.

The Midas Touch

Once the inventor made a machine
for making himself the happiest man in the world
only it worked best as a shoehorn.
Now, while all the other inventors
are busy building their wonderful machines
for the working of miracles,
the happy inventor is absorbed
in perfecting a device
for holding washing to a washing line.
At tea-time he uses a time machine
for a tea-strainer,
and yes, since you ask,
his marriage
is also a success.

Lennie

Lennie the roadsweeper being warned by my dad
if he ever caught him touching his children again
he'd kick him all the way from London to Brighton,
we, the snitching children, Father's own dear ones,

and the road to Brighton through Croydon and Purley,
out past the first cows and on to Redhill
and there in the distance the blue South Downs.
And I wondered which way Father would turn then,

would he kick Lennie up via Ditchling Beacon
or stick to the main road and come in at Patcham,
down through the chestnuts and onto the Steine,
and what they'd do when they reached the sea,

whether Father would just boot Lennie out into the blue
or whether they would go to the pub first,
one of those pubs where men patch up quarrels
and come out with their arms around each other?

The Hill

She turned at the top of the hill and looked back
a puddle of dogs at her feet
and drawing a joyful breath cried out
here, here he first had me...
meaning a long dead poet.
                    The land below was beet
where it wasn't fallow, and you could trace
the path up from the stile, the small blue car
tucked into the hedge, the boiled sweets
on the dashboard and the dog too sick to climb
lolloping about on the back seat.
                    Clouds
were coming in from Rotterdam across the sea,
the dogs were in raptures chasing rabbits
                    and I thought
how very likeable she was
for referring to her long dead poet like that,
and for throwing her military pants into the air
to his joy
while the planes droned over or fell in the sea.

Dylan Thomas in Later Years

Still sounding off, high-flown wag,
with the pencil-thin molls
from Arts Council and Academi
in the tired pubs around the BBC
and the tolerant late night bistros,
but bald now, and very fat indeed.

Still lapping it up, imperious old fart,
but no-one laughs any more
at the wardrobe ransacking trick,
lecturers wives no longer open their legs,
your cough is chronic and your cheeks
a different sort of red than youth's.

What happened that day in New York
and you coming round with a head
splitting but still functioning
to the words of a friend: *a record old boy...?*
I hardly think so... I hardly think so...
and you going on to prove it yourself.

A few scripts, a film that flopped,
another collection ('disappointing', TLS),
all those rhetorical stunts you pulled
still pored over by children in school
but a thing of the past - spare, clear, concise
patter a new generation of poets.

No, better the incompetent New York doctor,
you gone before your teeth, your hair,
before your gift, before the girls of summer,
tired of being pawed at, yawn your anecdotes away,
refuse another drink and suddenly
remember dinner-dates with Fenton, Raine.

fragment from The Editor Regrets

Dear Editor,
please consider the following poems for publication:
Homage to Wittgenstein, Double Helix and *Dusk: Mont St. Victoire.* I have been published in <u>The New Salon</u>, <u>Riposte</u> and <u>High Table</u>, and am featured in 'A Quorum of Poets' (University of Potsdam Press).
I look forward to hearing from you,
yours faithfully,
Allisdair Learning.

Dear Editor,
please consider the following poems for publication:
Shagging Melanie, Toxteth Nights and *Gary Mainlining.* I have been published in <u>Gob,</u> <u>Black Hole</u> and <u>Up Yours,</u> and am featured in 'A Six-Pack Of Poets' (Gutter Press).
I look forward to hearing from you,
yours faithfully,
Spud Payne.

Dear Editor,
please consider the following poems for publication:
Like Unto a Dream of Ancient Ways, Be Still Now My Heart and *Peace, Peace, the Moon Doth Shine.* I have been published in <u>The Inglenook</u>, <u>County Fair</u> and <u>The Beavers' Dam,</u> and am featured in 'A Nosegay of Poets' (Nutmeg Press).
I look forward to hearing from you,
yours faithfully,
Monica Feeling.

Death of an Old Man

Dying suited him, he looked illuminated,
like some old Irish saint set free
after a whole life consecrated
to God's Word and works of charity

except this was the 6th floor of the Heath
and digging drains was what he'd done.
Someone whistled down a corridor beneath
a bag of linen, a lift sighed open,

small things continued in the sort of way
he would have noted and approved
for he had cut a neat trench in his day
and cleanly had his shovel moved

for a good foreman and the going rate.
But now, his old head angled at the sun,
this man of betting shop, of bar and bedsit,
whose death would sell no late editions

was transfigured, and I knew then
as I tiptoed from the ward and down the hall
that simply to have lived beneath the sun
is epitaph sufficient for us all.

4am

Worried by love I woke alone at 4am
in the big bed that all afternoon
we'd played in, and thought of you
halfway across the sleeping town
lost to me among your own friends
and lovers, maybe. Leaping up
I tore the bed to bits and threw
your body scent behind the door
and changed the sheets, thinking
O not love again, and down the line
as sure as dawn, the end of love
and all that pain. The new sheets
smelled of Dreft and corner laundrette.
I missed your scent, I missed the sweat
and stains of our long afternoon,
I missed you, and lay till dawn
all sleepless with that living ache
you'd left me with, as keen to see you
as a teenager, yet as full of doom
as Lazarus being called to in his tomb.

Brasso

The day will come
when you will select a chair:
orthopaedic, posture-responsible,
maybe with a potty in it
and a footstool,
possibly with wheels.

A certain quantity
of hand-picked years will pass.
To give the chair
a thorough modernisation
would be the work of a moment
to your genius grandson:
hasn't he already modernised
trees, grass, cats and his own small sister?

but *Leonard*... you will say,
though this will not be his name,
just a little Brasso on the spokes
if you please...